THE CITY AND SUBURBAN VEGETABLE GARDEN

THE CLASSIC USDA FARMERS' BULLETIN NO. 936
WITH TIPS AND TRADITIONAL METHODS
IN SUSTAINABLE GARDENING AND PERMACULTURE

BY **U.S. DEPARTMENT OF AGRICULTURE**

ORIGINALLY PUBLISHED IN 1918

LEGACY EDITION
CLASSIC FARMERS BULLETIN LIBRARY
BOOK NO. 936

Doublebit Press
Eugene, OR

*New content, introduction, and annotations
Copyright © 2020 by Doublebit Press. All rights reserved.*

*Doublebit Press is an imprint of Eagle Nest Press
www.doublebitpress.com | Eugene, OR, USA*

*Original content under the public domain. Originally published in 1918 by the
U.S. Department of Agriculture.*

*This title, along with other Doublebit Press books including the Classic Farmers
Bulletin Library, are available at a volume discount for youth groups, outdoors
clubs, or reading groups.*

*Doublebit Press Legacy Edition ISBN
Paperback: 978-1-64389-141-5*

*Disclaimer: Because of its age and historic context, this book could contain
content on present-day inappropriate methods, activities, outdated medical
information, unsafe chemical and mechanical processes, or culturally and
racially insensitive content. Doublebit Press, or its employees, authors, and
other affiliates, assume no liability for any actions performed by readers or any
damages that might be related to information contained in this book. This text
has been published for historical study and for personal literary enrichment
toward the goal of preserving the American handcraft tradition, timeless trade
skills, and traditional artisanal knowledge.*

First Doublebit Press Legacy Edition Printing, 2020

Printed in the United States of America when purchased at retail in the USA

INTRODUCTION
Classic Farmers Bulletin Library

The old experts of artisanal trades, country and homestead knowledge, and the woods and mountains taught timeless principles and skills for centuries. Through their timeless books, the old experts offered rich descriptions of how the world works and encouraged learning through personal experiences *by doing*. Over the last 125 years, manufacturing, farming, and construction have substantially changed. Of course, many things have gotten simpler as equipment and technology have improved. In addition, some activities of pre-digital times are now no longer in vogue, or are even outright considered inappropriate or illegal. However, despite many of the positive changes in manufacturing and crafting methods that have occurred over the years, *there are many other skills and much knowledge that have been forgotten.*

By publishing the reprint series of the old USDA *Farmers' Bulletin*, it is our goal at Doublebit Press to do what we can to preserve and share the works from forgotten teachers that form the cornerstone of the history of the American artisans and traditional crafts. So much farm, homestead, and handcraft knowledge was passed to each generation through experience and hard work. An original mission of the US Department of Agriculture was to optimize farm outputs and increase the quality of life on farms through handcrafts, construction, and old-time farm tricks, tips, and skills. In their *Farmers' Bulletin* series, the USDA captured and passed on knowledge that applied to far more than just farmers!

Through remastered reprint editions of timeless classics, perhaps we can regain some of this lost knowledge for future generations. Today's interest in mastery of old handcraft skills, homestead self-sufficiency, and artisanal character has renewed an interest in the old arts. Luckily, the USDA's *Farmers' Bulletin* series contains thousands of pamphlets dedicated to teaching, improving life, and ensuring self-sufficiency to thrive in both the city and on a farm.

This book is an important contribution traditional handcraft and country skills literature and has important historical and collector value toward preserving the American handcraft and outdoors tradition. The knowledge it holds is an invaluable reference for practicing skills and hand craft methods. Its chapters thoroughly discuss some of the essential building blocks of knowledge that are fundamental but may have been forgotten as equipment gets fancier and technology gets smarter. In short, this reprint of the *Farmers' Bulletin* pamphlets was chosen for Legacy Edition printing because much of the basic skills and knowledge it contains has been forgotten or put to the wayside in trade for more modern conveniences and methods.

With technology playing a major role in everyday life, sometimes we need to take a step back in time to find those basic building blocks used for gaining mastery – the things that we have luckily not completely lost and has been recorded in books over the last two centuries. These skills aren't forgotten, they've just been shelved. *It's time to unshelve them once again and reclaim the lost knowledge of self-sufficiency.*

Based on this commitment to preserving our outdoors and handcraft artisanal heritage, we have taken great pride in publishing this book as a complete original work. We hope it is worthy of both study and collection by outdoors folk in the modern era of outdoors and traditional skills life.

Unlike many other photocopy reproductions of classic books that are common on the market, this Legacy Edition does not simply place poor photography of old texts on our pages and use error-prone optical scanning or computer-generated text. We want our work to speak for itself, and reflect the quality demanded by our customers who spend their hard-earned money. With this in mind, each Legacy Edition book that has been chosen for publication is carefully remastered from original print books, *with the Doublebit Legacy Edition printed and laid out in the exact way that it was presented at its original publication.* We provide a beautiful, memorable experience that is as true to the original text as best as possible, but with the aid of modern technology to make as beautiful a reading experience as possible for books that can be over a century old.

Because of its age and because it is presented in its original form, the book may contain misspellings, inking errors from print plates, and other printing blemishes that were common for the age. However, these are exactly the things that we feel give the book its character, which we preserved in this Legacy Edition. During digitization, we ensured that each illustration in the text was clean and sharp with the least amount of loss from being copied and digitized as possible. Full-page plate illustrations are presented as they were found, often including the extra blank page that was often behind a plate. For the covers, we use the original cover design to give the book its original feel. We are sure you'll appreciate the fine touches and attention to detail that your Legacy Edition has to offer.

For traditional handcrafters and classic artisanal enthusiasts who demand the best from their equipment, this Doublebit Press Legacy Edition reprint was made with you in mind. Both important and minor details have equally both been accounted for by our publishing staff, down to the cover, font, layout, and images. It is the goal of Doublebit Legacy Edition series to be worthy of collection in any outdoorsperson's library and that can be passed to future generations.

Every book selected to be in this series offers unique views and instruction on important skills, advice, tips, tidbits, anecdotes, stories, and experiences that will enrich the repertoire of any person who enjoys escaping a bit from today's modern technology-based, cookie-cutter, and highly industrialized skills. Instead, folks seeking to make things with their hands like the old days may find great value from these resurrected instructional manuals from the past. These books were not simply written to be shelved in a library – they contain our history and forgotten methods to make things with real character and energy with a *human* component.

Therefore, to learn the most basic building blocks of a craft leads to mastery of all its aspects. We hope this book helps you along this path with its rich descriptions and illustrations!

About the USDA Farmers' Bulletin Series

Back in the early 1900s, the US Department of Agriculture (USDA) began publication of small pamphlets that were meant to improve the outputs of America's farms, promote self-sufficiency, and help farmers and farming communities thrive. This publication series continued for decades, and volumes were always available when someone wanted to learn more about a specific skill or topic that could come in handy on the homestead.

Each of the 2,000+ volumes specializes in one specific topic, be it growing a certain crop, raising a particular animal, or building a type of farm structure. Each of the pamphlets captured the best knowledge available at that time, which often represented decades or centuries of old farmer knowledge, which we know, is incredibly useful and reliable!

As we continue to blaze paths into the digital frontier, many of these lost "farmers' tips" have become more useful than ever, particularly to folks looking to start homesteads and small-scale farms, as well as those who just want to live more sustainably, simply, and consciously in light of today's factory processed world. The *Farmers' Bulletin* is also highly useful for people who live in cities, as they contain much information for community gardens, urban and rooftop farming, and sustainable living tips.

Unfortunately, many of these print volumes of the *Farmers' Bulletin* are now out of print. Indeed, because these texts are in the public domain, they are easily found and are available on the Internet. However, many of these books that are easily found on the web are often low-resolution photocopies, complete with scribble marks or other distracting spots. For the first time, high-quality, professionally restored *Farmers' Bulletin* reissues are being made by Doublebit Press to increase access to the timeless knowledge that each contains.

This Doublebit Press Legacy Edition republishes this tradition of handcrafted quality and artisanal work. We hope that this deluxe printed edition of this book will help you gain mastery in your craft, as it is presented in the exact form that it was originally published. Even today, the knowledge contained within its pages are timeless and have much to teach!

Finally, as works of art, the USDA *Farmers' Bulletin* issues contain beautiful illustrations and line art that are a sign of simpler, yet authentic times when quality mattered and craftsmanship was king. This collectible volume makes a great addition to the bookshelf of any handcrafter, maker, artisan, farmer, homesteader, or outdoors enthusiast!

Enjoy some old-time, vintage charm when the government actually encouraged you to be self-sufficient with these beautifully illustrated and classic instruction manuals by the USDA!

THE CITY AND SUBURBAN VEGETABLE GARDEN

H. M. CONOLLY
Assistant Horticulturist in Agricultural Education

A Typical City Garden

FARMERS' BULLETIN 936
UNITED STATES DEPARTMENT OF AGRICULTURE

Contribution from the Bureau of Plant Industry
WM. A. TAYLOR, Chief

and the

States Relations Service
A. C. TRUE, Chief

Washington, D. C.   February, 1918

Show this bulletin to a neighbor. Additional copies may be obtained free from the Division of Publications, United States Department of Agriculture

THIS BULLETIN is intended primarily to show the importance of gardening in city and suburban districts and to encourage greater efforts in these sections.

City gardening in back yards and vacant lots may be made the source of considerable profit and furnishes healthful exercise for the members of the family.

Gardening under the conditions that exist in cities and towns is essentially different from gardening in the country, in that city people as a rule are not experienced in the art of growing plants.

Proper organization and instruction are essential to get the most out of city gardening. In the following pages suggestions are given for conducting the work of organization, as well as directions covering the preparation of the soil, the starting of plants, and the cultivation and care of all the more important garden crops.

THE CITY AND SUBURBAN VEGETABLE GARDEN.

CONTENTS.

	Page.		Page.
Importance of city gardens	3	Plants	17
Types of gardening	5	Hotbeds and cold frames	18
Cost and value of crops from home gardens	7	Fertilizing the garden	22
Labor and expense required to make home gardens	8	Liming	24
		Preparing the soil	25
Location and soil	10	Time of planting	28
Size of the garden	12	Setting plants	31
Arrangement of the garden	12	Cultivation	32
Fences and windbreaks	14	Irrigation	33
Succession of crops	14	Control of insects and diseases	33
Rotations	15	Saving surplus vegetables	34
Seed	15	Directions for growing vegetable crops	35

IMPORTANCE OF CITY GARDENS.

A WELL-PLANNED and carefully tended garden is one of the most pleasant and satisfying pieces of work in which the city or suburban family can utilize its spare time. If the soil is properly prepared and a little attention is given the garden as required, the work need not become a burden on the members of the household.

Gardening the back yards and vacant lots of the cities and towns of our country is a worthy endeavor, because it utilizes the spare

FIG. 1.—A group of vegetables harvested at one time from a home garden.

time and labor of persons employed at other work and brings to the family table a greater diversity of food. (Fig. 1.) It also eliminates many undesirable views and eyesores, putting in their places pleasing green growing crops. (Figs. 2 and 3 and title-page illustration.)

Gardening is a patriotic work which will result in both pleasure and profit. It gives pleasure not only in the work with the growing plants, but in the producing of high-quality, crisp, fresh vegetables for the family table. It gives profit by producing vegetables cheaper than they can be purchased and by reducing the need for more expensive foods. (Fig. 4.) Gardening is profitable also because better health is secured by the exercise in the open air and the use of more vegetables in the diet.

Gardening should be an important part of the city and suburban life because of the interest it adds to the lives of people little used to country surroundings. It is interesting to the young and the old, and to women and girls as well as men and boys. There is no better way to keep the boys off the streets and out of mischief than to give them a plat of ground on which they can make a garden (figs. 5 and 6), the results to be their very own. Very young children (fig. 7) can be interested in garden work. One 5-year-old boy in Wash-

FIG. 2.—A city lot which may be used for a garden.

ington, D. C., this past season planted several kinds of seed and grew the plants to maturity. This youngster could be sent to the garden for any one of half a dozen different vegetables and would return with the right one.

TYPES OF GARDENING.

There are several types of gardening which should be of interest in all city and suburban sections. Some of the more important types are back-yard gardens, vacant-lot gardens, and school gardens.

The back-yard garden is probably the most important of the three, because it is more intimately associated with the home. The area

FIG. 3.—A vacant lot the first season after the rubbish had been cleared away and a garden established.

immediately back of the house is the plat usually considered as the back-yard garden. If this spot is not used as a garden it often becomes an unsightly place, and thus gardening improves the home surroundings. (Figs. 8 and 9.)

The condition of the soil in the back yard can be steadily improved year after year as long as the family occupies the house. (Fig. 10.) Its nearness to the house is a great inducement for the family to work the garden and to utilize the crops to the fullest extent.

Vacant-lot gardens are important because of the large areas that can be found for the work.

Commercial truck growers or market gardeners utilize land in the outskirts of cities, but unless this land is very productive or can be had at a low rental for a period of years it will not pay them to lease it. With the use of the home gardener's labor, however, the cropping of these areas can be made remunerative.

Large areas of vacant land may be taken over by a company or organization and divided into a number of small plats which individuals may tend. In some cases large plats have been used as gardens by a number of individuals who shared equally in the labor, expense, and results. This type of community garden is not usually a success unless it can be done by a school or institution which controls all of the work. Figure 11 shows a large area which has been divided into a number of individual gardens, while figure 12 shows a large area used as a garden by a public institution.

School gardens are important because they bring to the child early in life an opportunity to see how plants grow, to identify the kinds of plants that are found in the garden, and to learn some of the economic phases of gardening as applied to the family food supply. (Fig. 13.)

FIG. 4.—A vacant lot after plowing. Four women removed the stones and trash from this plat, planted garden crops, and produced enough vegetables for their families.

Porch and window gardens are not important, but in some of the thickly populated sections of the larger cities this type of gardening is quite often practiced. Window boxes, boxes at the ends of porches or on shed roofs, boxes on the edges of walks or even on the small front lawn, and boxes and barrels on the roofs of tenement and apartment buildings are some of the ways of utilizing small spaces in the growing of plants. In the limited areas of boxes, barrels, etc. (figs. 14 and 15), no large quantity of food can be produced, but the growing of plants can be made an interesting study, besides adding something to the family table. Lettuce, parsley, radishes, onions, and tomatoes are some of the crops best suited for such limited spaces.

Both boys' and girls' clubs and adult clubs may utilize vacant lots or the home back yards. There are a number of kinds of clubs besides regular garden clubs which have accomplished wonderful results in garden work. (Fig. 16.) Boy-scout troops, girl-scout troops, woodcraft clubs, and other similar organizations are among this class of clubs.

COST AND VALUE OF CROPS FROM HOME GARDENS.

There is a great lack of uniformity in figures collected on the value of garden crops. Prices vary from day to day and also vary in different sections of a city. Some persons figure the value of

FIG. 5.—A lot covered with rubbish. Enthusiasm and labor were required to make this plat into a garden.

their garden products at the highest retail prices; others at wholesale prices. Many children obtain prices for their garden products much greater than market prices.

To give uniformity to the value of garden vegetables, a scale of prices should be established for the city, and all who make records of their gardens should use as a guide the scale set for their city.

The following items of cost and valuation of garden products are offered as suggestions to those interested in gardening campaigns.

Cost of fertilizer, labor, tools, seeds, plants, and spraying material.

(a) Fertilizers: Charge manure at $2.50 per 1½ cubic yards or 2-horse load. This would be equal to two 1-horse loads. Commercial fertilizer and lime should be charged at cost price.

(b) Labor: Include all expense of labor hired.
(c) Tools: Charge at one-fourth the first cost when new.
(d) Seeds: All seeds should be charged at prices at store, whether saved, kept over, or given to you.
(e) Plants: Charge at market prices.
(f) Spraying material: Charge at cost price.

Value of crops.

The value of crops should be figured at the prices given below if of good quality; if not of good quality, reduce the value accordingly. If of extra size and quality or extra early, increase the value.

Beans, Lima (shelled beans), 25 cents per quart.
Beans, snap, 30 cents per peck.
Beets, 50 cents per peck. (50 beets of medium size.)
Cabbages, 5 cents per head.
Cauliflower, 10 cents per head; large, high quality, up to 20 cents.
Carrots, 50 cents per peck. (80 carrots of medium size.)
Celery, 4 cents per stalk.
Sweet corn, 2 cents per ear.
Cucumbers, 2 cents each for large and 50 cents per peck for small pickles.
Eggplants, 5 cents each.
Lettuce, 5 cents per head, or an equal quantity of leaf lettuce.
Muskmelons, 10 cents each.
Onions, 35 cents per peck, dry; 20 cents per quart, for sets; 5 cents a bunch if green.
Parsnips, 40 cents per peck.
Peas, 40 cents per peck.
Peppers, 10 cents per dozen.
Irish potatoes:
    Early, 35 cents per peck.
    Late, 25 cents per peck.
Radishes, 3 cents per bunch.
Salsify, 50 cents per peck.
Spinach, kale, turnip greens, beet greens, mustard, etc., 25 cents per peck.
Squashes:
    Summer, 50 cents per dozen.
    Late, 25 cents each.
Tomatoes:
    Early, 50 cents per peck.
    Main crop, 25 cents per peck.
Turnips, 25 cents per peck.
Watermelons, 25 cents each.

LABOR AND EXPENSE REQUIRED TO MAKE HOME GARDENS.

Persons interested in making a garden often ask how much labor it will take to care properly for a garden of a certain size, and what results should be expected under average conditions.

The following records secured in the District of Columbia are thoroughly reliable and vouched for by the school teachers and leaders who supervised part of the work and by the agricultural agent for the District:

THE CITY AND SUBURBAN VEGETABLE GARDEN. 9

(1) Records from 20 school boys' and girls' home gardens, each of which comprised an area of 500 square feet or more.

> Average area per garden, 1,022 square feet.
> Average expense per garden, $1.38.
> Average hours of labor per garden, 17.

(2) Records from 59 school boys' and girls' home gardens, each of which comprised an area less than 500 square feet.

> Average area per garden, 166 square feet.
> Average expense per garden, 62 cents.
> Average hours of labor per garden, 14.

(3) Records from 8 club boys' and girls' home gardens, each of which comprised an area more than 500 square feet.

> Average area per garden, 1,909 square feet.
> Average expense per garden, $2.51.
> Average hours of labor per garden, 39.

(4) Records from 12 club boys' and girls' home gardens, each of which comprised an area less than 500 square feet.

> Average area per garden, 305 square feet.
> Average expense per garden, 84 cents.
> Average hours of labor per garden, 28.

(5) Records from 50 family home gardens, which comprised areas ranging from 720 to 65,340 square feet.

> Average area per garden, 7,801 square feet.
> Average expense per garden, $13.92.
> Average hours of labor per garden, 132.

From the above records from 149 home gardens, a garden averaging 2,800 square feet will cost $4.82 and will require about 58 hours of labor to take care of it during the season.

The figures in the following table are taken from the records referred to above.

Value of vegetables which a home garden will produce.

Kind of garden.	Number.	Average per garden.				Value per square foot.		Value per acre.	
		Area.	Expense.	Value.	Hours of work.	Gross.	Net.	Gross.	Net.
Boys' and girls' home school gardens:		*Sq. ft.*							
More than 500 square feet in area	20	1,022	$1.38	$7.50	17	$0.00734	$0.006	$319.73	$261.36
Less than 500 square feet in area	59	166	.62	2.97	14	.018	.0142	784.08	618.55
Boys' and girls' club gardens:									
More than 500 square feet in area	8	1,909	2.51	14.46	39	.0122	.0092	531.43	400.75
Less than 500 square feet in area	12	305	.84	6.95	28	.0226	.0197	984.46	858.13
Family home gardens:									
Ranging from 720 to 65,340 square feet	50	7,801	13.92	70.56	132	.00904	.00726	393.78	316.25
Best garden of large extent	1	8,800	25.00	231.82	200	.0263	.0236	1,194.98	1,067.22
Best garden of small extent	1	272	.85	9.05	17½	.033	.03	1,437.48	1,306.80

The figures in this table show that the average net value per acre is considerably greater in the gardens of 500 square feet or less than in larger areas. This is shown both in the case of the boys' and girls' home school gardens and in the boys' and girls' home club gardens.

Another convincing point the figures make is that the club gardens produced very much better returns than the home school gardens or the home family gardens. This difference is due, no doubt, to the better supervision given to the club gardens and the greater stimulation due to healthy competition among the members.

LOCATION AND SOIL.

If no yard is available, a suitable vacant lot may be secured. In every case the garden should be near the house, so that it will be possible for the housewife to go into the garden and in a few minutes secure the desired vegetables. When the garden is situated at some distance from the house the effort necessary to care for it becomes a burden, the products are not utilized to the fullest extent, and the garden is soon neglected.

Areas shaded a large portion of the time should not be selected for a garden. (Fig. 17.) The foliage crops, such as lettuce, parsley, and chard, will thrive fairly well when they get three or four hours of sunlight a day. Such crops as tomatoes, eggplants, and peppers

FIG. 6.—The same plat illustrated in figure 5, showing a very profitable vegetable garden maintained by boys assisted by their parents.

Fig. 7.—An example of how children may be interested in garden work. This 3-year-old youngster has spent many hours in the garden and can name many of the matured crops.

should have an abundance of sunshine, at least five or six hours each day. (Fig. 18.)

Most city gardeners are handicapped in that they must make the best of the space and soil available to them. While a sandy loam with a well-drained southern exposure will give better results than less favored locations, the gardener should not be deterred from making an effort even though his location is not the best.

Almost any kind of soil, unless it is composed of bricks, mortar, stone, rubbish, etc., can be used for gardening if it is properly handled. Heavy clay soils may be improved greatly by adding large quantities of strawy manure in the fall or by turning under green-manure crops. It is usually practicable to cover the clay soil with 2 or 3 inches of sifted coal ashes and then thoroughly incorporate the two by spading and hoeing. Sandy soils may be decidedly improved for gardening purposes by growing green-manure crops on the land or by turning under liberal quantities of stable manure.

Good drainage is very important in the garden, and if the soil is not naturally well drained it should be drained artificially. Tile drains are most satisfactory for the garden, but open ditches may be used.

SIZE OF THE GARDEN.

The city back yard is seldom large enough to produce sufficient vegetables for the average family. On limited areas of 800 square feet or less, only such crops as lettuce, snap beans, onions, radishes, a few tomato plants, spinach, kale, chard, beets, and other crops requiring little space should be grown. (Fig. 19.) Where more space is available, a quarter acre may be profitably employed, and where sweet corn and sweet and Irish potatoes are to be grown a half acre is none too much. (Fig. 20.) The keynote to success in the garden is to have the soil as fertile as possible, so as to produce sufficient vegetables with the least amount of labor.

FIG. 8.—A back yard after being cleaned up and planted to early Irish potatoes.

A small garden well cared for is far better than a larger garden which is neglected.

ARRANGEMENT OF THE GARDEN.

The arrangement of the garden should be carefully worked out to suit the conditions of each particular garden. In the winter, when there is usually plenty of time available, it is a good plan to sit down with paper, pencil, and rule and draw up a plan of the garden. Mark on this plan the location for each vegetable and the area covered, the successions, date of planting, etc. By making a plan and following it throughout the season the greatest success will be had with the garden.

While each garden must be planned to suit the conditions, there are a few general rules which apply to all gardens. The rows should run north and south, to give the best distribution of sunlight on all sides of the plants, but where it is more convenient, and where washing must be prevented, the rows can run in other directions. All permanent vegetables, such as rhubarb, asparagus, and herbs, should be planted at one side of the garden, where they will not be disturbed every year. Tall vegetables, like corn and pole beans, should be put in a position where they will not shade the small vegetables. Wherever the land is available and horse cultivation can be used, allow

FIG. 9.—The same area shown in figure 8 later in the season. Beans, chard, and cabbages have followed the potatoes, and Lima beans have covered the board fence.

sufficient space between rows for the larger cultivating tools. Also run the rows the long way of the garden in order to avoid excessive turning at the ends of the rows. (Fig. 21.) For horse cultivation provide a 4 or 5 foot pathway along two sides of the garden at right angles to the rows, so that turning with the cultivator can be managed without injuring the vegetables. All vegetables that are to be planted early and that require early cultivation should be grouped at one side of the garden, to facilitate cultivation. Figure 22 may offer many suggestions as to the arrangement and location of the crops in a quarter-acre garden. The distances given for rows are for horse cultivation.

FENCES AND WINDBREAKS.

Every garden should be surrounded by a fence to keep out stray dogs, cats, chickens, and small children. In the prairie regions a windbreak or shelter belt is absolutely necessary to protect the garden, and in other regions, while not so necessary, a windbreak may protect the crops from damage by strong winds, and the protection from cold winds may lengthen the crop-growing season considerably. If buildings, a grove of trees, a row of evergreens, or a hedge are not available as a windbreak, a tight board fence may be erected, which will serve the double purpose of a fence and a windbreak.

SUCCESSION OF CROPS.

To make a garden yield the maximum quantity of vegetables it is necessary that the land be occupied as much of the time as possible. In some sections three or more crops may be grown on the same land during the season. (Fig. 23.) Care must be used in selecting the crops that are to follow the early-season crops. The vegetable used for the first planting, or one with the same characters or belonging to the same family, should not be used in the same place at the second planting. Cabbage, kale, mustard, Brussels sprouts, and

FIG. 10.—A portion of a prize-winning garden in Washington, D. C. This garden soil has been improved every year for a period of five years. The value of the crop in 1917 was at the rate of $1,149.98 per acre on an area of 8,800 square feet.

FIG. 11.—A portion of a large field which has been divided into a number of individual gardens. Each garden is 25 by 40 feet. The plat in the foreground was planted entirely to tomatoes. Many such fields may be plowed and put under cultivation as vegetable gardens.

cauliflower should not follow each other, for the same insects and diseases affect all these plants; and for the same reason peppers, eggplants, and tomatoes should not follow each other. In many cases, especially in the more southern sections of the country, after an early vegetable is harvested, if no other vegetable is to be planted until autumn, the ground may be planted with cowpeas or some other leguminous crop which can be turned under in preparing for the fall crop.

ROTATIONS.

The rotation of crops is very important in the garden, both in conserving plant food and in checking the spread of insects and diseases. Space which has been occupied by a diseased crop should not be replanted the following year with the same or a closely related crop. It is a good plan to rotate the entire garden every year with an equal-sized plat which has been planted to clover or cowpeas. (Fig. 24.) If such an extra plat is not available, the locations of the various vegetables may be changed each succeeding year. Following root crops, such as parsnips, beets, and carrots, with foliage crops, like kale, cabbage, collards, and lettuce, or with crops like tomatoes, beans, melons, or peppers, will tend to conserve the plant food in the soil and prevent heavy infestations of insects and plant diseases.

SEED.

As soon as the location for the garden is selected and a plan made showing the kinds of vegetables to be grown and the places for planting them, the question of varieties should be decided. A number of points should be considered in selecting the varieties to grow, among them being the time of maturity, the adaptation of the variety to the local conditions, and the quality of the vegetable produced. Usually it is better to select only standard varieties that do well in the locality, but a few novelties may be tried in a small way. With the exception of tomatoes and corn it is often better to select a few varieties and plant these in succession than to procure a larger number of early and late varieties.

Vegetable seed should be purchased several weeks ahead of the time it is to be used, and it is advisable to procure the seed only from reliable seedsmen. A good plan is to procure several descriptive catalogues either from reliable local seedsmen or from other

FIG. 12.—An area devoted to vegetables at an industrial school for girls.

good seed houses. These catalogues should be secured in the winter, so that the selection of seed may be made at leisure moments and the order sent out early.

The quantity of seed to purchase will depend upon the preferences for different vegetables and the size of the garden. The table on page 28 gives the amount of seed necessary for a 50-foot row of the various garden crops.

Buy only first-class seed, for inferior seed will be expensive at any price. Buy only the quantity of seed actually needed for your garden. To buy more may deprive another of a garden.

THE CITY AND SUBURBAN VEGETABLE GARDEN. 17

Seed which has been left from the preceding season should be tested by counting out 25 to 50 seeds of each variety, putting them in a plate between two sheets of moist cloth or blotting paper, and covering with another plate. By looking at the seed every day, the promptness and percentage of germination can be ascertained. Good grades of most garden seeds should germinate 60 to 85 per cent in five or six days. Seeds that send out strong sprouts in a few days have the vitality necessary to insure a good stand of plants, and this is an important item in garden work.

PLANTS.

Plants for the garden can be grown in a limited way in shallow boxes or flats set in a sunny window of the dwelling house. (Fig.

FIG. 13.—A city lot made into a school garden. The children work the garden under the supervision of the teacher. This garden during the season of 1917 produced vegetables to the value of $125.

25.) The soil for the seed boxes should be fine and mellow, and the seed should be planted in rows, with a label to designate each variety or kind. As soon as the plants form three or four leaves they should be transplanted into other boxes, the plants being set at least 2 inches apart each way. Where there is not sufficient space in the house for growing all the plants desired, it is possible to grow the seedlings inside and transplant them into a coldframe out of doors.

All seedlings grown in boxes or flats should be transplanted at least once before they are ready to set in the garden. This transplanting causes the plant to become stocky and to produce a mass of fine roots. (Fig. 26.) In many cases the seedlings are transplanted from the seed flats into earthen pots or dirt bands. Plants from the pots or bands can be set in the garden without disturbing the roots, and the plants receive no check in their growth. By this means it is possible to have plants ready to set in the garden at any time when another crop is taken out. For example, as fast as early cabbages are cut, tomato plants can be set in their places, and pepper plants may be set in the row as fast as the early lettuce is harvested, etc.

HOTBEDS AND COLDFRAMES.

A hotbed and a coldframe of some form are very necessary to secure the maximum benefits from the garden. Plants can be

FIG. 14.—Barrels utilized for growing vegetables. These were filled two-thirds full of ashes, and a foot of soil on top was supplied by a gardener who had time and energy to devote to a very limited area in a congested section of Washington, D. C.

raised more satisfactorily and on a much larger scale with frames than with seed boxes set in the house window. The frames can also be used for maturing early crops and for carrying over crops into the winter.

A very serviceable frame for a hotbed or coldframe may be constructed like the one shown in figure 27. Oak or cypress boards 1 inch thick may be used. A more permanent frame can be constructed by using concrete. A hotbed 6 by 6 feet will be sufficient for the needs of most home gardens, and a coldframe of equal size will be found of great assistance in growing crops successfully.

MAKING A HOTBED.

To make a hotbed, secure a quantity of fresh horse manure, consisting of about two parts of the solid excrement to one part of litter. Pile in a heap under cover for a few days, so that it will heat, and turn it over a few times to mix it thoroughly. When mixed, place the manure in a pile to a depth of 18 inches, keeping it well trampled while being placed. On top of this manure place the frame and pack manure tightly all around it. Place inside the frame 3 to 4 inches of rich soil and cover with a glass sash. Window sash can often be used for this purpose. The bed should stand for several days, some ventilation being given meanwhile,

FIG. 15.—The other side of the yard seen in figure 14. For several months this garden supplied two elderly people with fresh vegetables.

so that the gases from the manure may escape. When the temperature of the bed has fallen to between 80° and 90° F., the seed may be planted.

Another very satisfactory method of constructing a hotbed is to dig a pit to a depth of 18 to 24 inches and in this pack the manure and place the frame over it. This method has the advantage of requiring less manure. In using either method it is a good plan in the fall to cover the ground where the hotbed is to be located with a layer of manure about a foot thick. This covering will keep the soil soft and warm, which will be a great aid when the time comes to construct the hotbed

Fig. 16.—A 10-year-old boy in his club garden containing 272 square feet. The result of his labor was $9.05 worth of vegetables.

A hotbed may often be constructed adjoining the house and a pipe from the house heating system used to furnish heat for the bed.

MANAGEMENT OF A HOTBED.

When the temperature of a hotbed has fallen to the required degree, the soil is raked until very fine and all strawy material and refuse removed. The seed is planted in rows 3 inches apart and to a depth of an eighth to a half inch, according to the size of the seed. A thin stick or a lath can be pressed into the soil to give the required depth and to mark the rows. The seed should be covered very lightly with soil.

As the plants grow, they should be watered often enough to keep the soil from drying out, but not enough to keep the soil water-soaked. Water should be applied in a fine spray, and this can be done by using a fine sprinkler on the hose or watering can. The watering should be done early in the day, so that the plants will have time to dry off before night.

Plants should have plenty of fresh air, but should not receive a direct draft or air that is chilly enough to check their growth. The hotbed sash may be raised slightly in the morning after the air becomes warm, but it should be lowered again before it turns cold toward evening. The sash should be opened only on the side opposite from the direction of the wind. On a bright sunny day the sash may be raised several inches, but on a dull day only a very small opening should be made. Always give good ventilation after watering the plants. When the plants become large and the weather is warm, the sash is left off gradually for longer periods, in order to harden the plants.

Such plants as are being grown for setting in the garden should be transplanted into the coldframe as soon as they are about 2 inches high and have three or four leaves. Plants which are to mature crops in the hotbed should be thinned out as soon as they begin to crowd in the row. The soil should be stirred several times and all weeds taken out as soon as they appear. A hand weeder is a useful tool for this purpose.

Radish, lettuce, onions, etc., can be produced very early in the spring in the hotbed. Tomato, cabbage, celery, cauliflower, eggplant, pepper, and kohl-rabi plants should be started in the hotbed in order to have them ready for planting in early spring.

USE OF COLDFRAMES.

A coldframe usually is only a sash-covered frame placed over a portion of good garden soil. No heat is supplied except what comes from the sun. A coldframe is used to protect tender plants during the early spring or late autumn. The management of a coldframe is very similar to that of a hotbed both in regard to watering and in ventilating.

FIG. 17.—An area completely shaded for more than three or four hours of the day. Such areas should never be planted.

FERTILIZING THE GARDEN.

The soil used for growing vegetables should be very rich and well supplied with humus. To produce vegetables of high quality and in a short period of time it is necessary to have large amounts of readily available plant food. Well-rotted stable manure is probably the best fertilizer, because it supplies both the plant food and humus. Wherever it is possible to obtain sufficient manure it should be applied at the rate of 1 to 2 pounds per square foot or a good wheelbarrow load or two to each square rod, depending on the character of the soil. If sufficient manure is not obtainable it can be supplemented by using commercial fertilizer. An application of 3 to 6 pounds per

FIG. 18.—An area which receives more than five hours' sunlight in a day. Such areas can be made into successful gardens.

square rod of a high-grade mixture analyzing 8 to 10 per cent phosphoric acid, 2 to 4 per cent nitrogen, and 1 to 3 per cent potash will be satisfactory on many garden soils.

Prepared sheep manure is an excellent fertilizer if it can be obtained at a reasonable price. Nitrate of soda is often used to hasten the growth of some plants. The best method of using nitrate of soda is to dissolve a teaspoonful in a gallon of water and use the solution to water the plants. Do not sprinkle nitrate of soda water over the leaves of the plants, for concentrated solutions are likely to burn the leaves.

When coarse or strawy manure is used it should be applied and plowed under in the fall, but if the stable manure is well rotted it may be applied as a top-dressing and plowed under in the spring. Commercial fertilizer may be applied broadcast over the land after spading and thoroughly mixed with the soil by hoeing and raking, or it may be applied under the row.

A compost heap will furnish plant food that is in a quickly available condition and also soil which can be used in the hotbed, coldframe, and seed flats, and to put under and around plants which require considerable quantities of nitrogen. Such plants as cucumbers, cantaloupes, watermelons, and squashes will be greatly benefited if good compost is used in the hill when the seed is planted.

A compost heap can be easily made. First, select a place near the garden, but screened from view. Put down a layer of sods and over

FIG. 19.—A limited space which may be planted to crops such as tomatoes, cabbage, lettuce, snap beans, beets, kale, and radish, with Lima beans on the fence.

this place alternate layers of manure, sandy soil, and clay soil until the pile is of the desired height. The whole compost pile should be cut down and turned several times during the season, and by the next spring the manure will be thoroughly decayed and mixed with the soil. In the more thickly populated sections of a city compost heaps are not usually allowed, so compost or decayed manure will have to be hauled in from out of the city.

It is often possible for the manure from city stables to be collected, taken to dumps located in the suburbs, and there composted. From this source city gardeners may be supplied.

FIG. 20.—A large area which may be planted to crops that require plenty of room. This garden is planted to sweet corn, peas, sweet potatoes, peppers, etc.

The supply of commercial fertilizer should be conserved to the utmost. A satisfactory fertilizer may be had by using 40 pounds of chicken or pigeon manure, both of which are especially rich in nitrogen, 5 to 8 pounds of unleached hardwood ashes, and 5 to 8 pounds of acid phosphate per square rod. The chicken or pigeon manure should be applied separately, as a loss of nitrogen will result if it is mixed with the other ingredients. Many homes burn sufficient wood to produce the necessary quantity of ashes, and comparatively little care is required to collect and save them, while chicken manure is available to most gardeners. Acid phosphate is relatively cheap and comparatively plentiful, but if so desired bone meal may be substituted for it.

LIMING.

Lime added to the soil will help to break up the soil particles and will also correct any acid or sour condition. Lime is not a plant food, but it aids in making the plant food in the soil more available.

Lime may be applied to the soil in the form of burned lime, hydrated lime, or finely ground limestone. Finely ground limestone may be applied either in the fall or in the spring. Burned lime or hydrated lime should not be applied in connection with stable manure because it liberates a great deal of the ammonia in the manure. The manure may be spread on the land and spaded or plowed under. The lime may be scattered over the spaded soil and worked in by hoeing and raking, or by harrowing. If the manure is applied in the fall the lime may be applied in the spring.

From 5 to 8 pounds per square rod of burned lime or hydrated lime will be a sufficient application and may be repeated every three or four years.

Although a garden soil may be tested with litmus paper to see if it is in need of lime, a good plan for most gardeners is to use lime anyway. Lime is comparatively cheap, and for the limited areas of most city gardens the expense will be small.

PREPARING THE SOIL.

The garden soil should be thoroughly prepared. A deep seed bed (8 to 10 inches) with the soil loose and mellow to the full depth is very essential. Heavy lands should be plowed or spaded in the fall

FIG. 21.—Long straight rows of vegetables which add attractiveness to a garden and lessen the labor of cultivation. Note how this garden has produced these results.

if there is no danger of washing and replowed or dug up with a mattock in the spring. Land that it is not advisable to plow in the fall should be plowed as early in the spring as possible. If there is plenty of humus in the soil or some green-manure crop is turned under, the soil will crumble and a fine seed bed can be easily prepared. If the soil is heavy and is lacking in humus it is inclined to stick together and bake, and it is a difficult matter to pulverize it sufficiently for gardening work. Care must be used to cover all sod and strawy material, so they will quickly decay and not interfere with garden operations.

Often the ground of back yards or vacant lots selected for gardens has been hardened by much trampling, and the soil can not be put

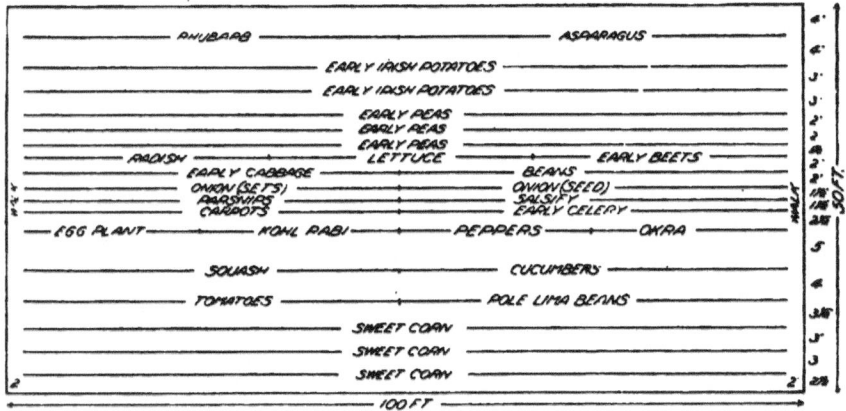

FIG. 22.—Diagram showing the location and arrangement of crops in a garden about a quarter of an acre in area.

into proper condition without the expenditure of considerable labor. The task of digging up such soil for the first time is very arduous, but it does not pay to slight the work. Spading to a depth of 8 inches and loosening 2 inches below the spade depth is very essential. Fining the soil all the way is also necessary.

TOOLS.

A spade or spading fork, a hoe, a rake, a dibble or trowel, and a line are the essential tools required for a small garden. There are a few more tools, however, which are very desirable for certain kinds of work. Some of these tools are a mattock, a garden hose or a watering can, a wheelbarrow, a shovel, a hand weeder of some form, and a hand wheel cultivator. Some of the tools mentioned are shown in figures 28, 29, and 30.

LAYING OFF.

It is a simple matter to take the plan which has been made of the garden and lay off the distance on the opposite sides of the garden and set a stake at each place. By stretching a line between the stakes it is possible to secure straight rows, which add attractiveness to the garden. Straight, long rows are usually the first points to be noticed by any judge of a garden.

SEEDING.

In a small vegetable garden the seed is sown by hand, and with such crops as lettuce, radishes, onions, and beets is sown thicker

FIG. 23.—An illustration of companion plantings and succession of crops. Radishes are shown planted between onions and sweet corn (not yet up) between snap beans. All the area was later planted to navy beans.

than the plants need to be, so as to insure a stand. Later, the extra plants are removed, leaving only the strongest and best. Extreme care should be taken to use no more seed than absolutely necessary. The usual tendency is to sow too thickly. All small seed is sown to a depth of a quarter to three-quarters of an inch, depending upon the soil and the season, while larger seeds, like corn, beans, and peas, are sown to a depth of 2 inches.

A CITY GARDENER'S PLANTING TABLE.

Distances apart for rows and plants, depths of planting, quantity of seeds and number of plants required for 50 feet of row, and time required for growth.

Kind of vegetable.	Distance apart.		Depth for planting seed.	Seed and plants for 50 feet of row.		Time until ready for use (days).
	Rows.	Plants in the row.		Seed.	Plants.	
			Inches.			
Asparagus	2 feet	15 inches	1 to 1½	½ ounce	30 to 40	
Bean:						
Bush	do	3 to 4 inches	1½ to 2	½ pint		40 to 65
Bush Lima	2½ feet	6 to 10 inches	1½ to 2	¼ to ½ pint		70 to 90
Pole Lima	3 feet	3 to 4 feet	1½ to 2	¼ pint		80 to 120
Beet	15 to 18 inches	4 to 5 inches	1 to 1½	1 ounce		60 to 80
Cabbage	2 to 2½ feet	15 to 20 inches	½	¼ ounce	30 to 45	90 to 130
Carrot	15 to 18 inches	3 to 4 inches	½	½ ounce		70 to 100
Cauliflower	2 to 2½ feet	15 to 18 inches	½	1/16 ounce	30 to 40	100 to 130
Celery	18 to 24 inches	4 to 6 inches	⅛	do	100 to 125	120 to 150
Collard	do	12 to 18 inches	½	¼ ounce	30 to 50	100 to 120
Corn, sweet	2½ to 3 feet	10 to 12 inches	2	⅛ pint		60 to 100
Cucumber	4 to 5 feet	15 inches	1 to 1½	¼ ounce		60 to 80
Eggplant	2 to 2½ feet	18 to 24 inches	½	⅛ ounce	25 to 35	100 to 140
Kale	18 to 24 inches	8 to 10 inches	½	¼ ounce		90 to 120
Lettuce	15 to 18 inches	6 to 10 inches	½	do	60 to 100	60 to 90
Melons:						
Muskmelon	5 to 6 feet	Drills 18 inches; Hills 5 feet	1 to 1½	do		120 to 150
Watermelon	8 to 10 feet	Drills 2 to 3 feet; Hills 8 feet	1 to 2	½ ounce		100 to 120
Okra	3 feet	2 feet	1 to 2	1 ounce		90 to 140
Onion:						
Seed	15 inches	3 to 4 inches	½ to 1	½ ounce		130 to 150
Sets	do	do	1 to 2	¼ quart		60 to 120
Parsley	do	do	¼	¼ ounce		90 to 120
Parsnip	15 to 18 inches	do	½ to 1	¼ ounce		125 to 160
Pea	2½ to 3 feet	1 inch	2 to 3	½ to 1 pint		40 to 80
Potatoes:						
Irish	2 to 2½ feet	12 to 18 inches	4	2 to 3 lbs.		80 to 140
Sweet	4 to 5 feet	14 to 18 inches	2 to 3	2 pounds	(1)	140 to 160
Radish	12 to 15 inches	1 inch	½ to 1	½ ounce		20 to 140
Salsify	15 to 18 inches	1 to 2 inches	½ to 1	do		120 to 180
Spinach	do	do	1 to 2	do		30 to 60
Squash:						
Bush	3 to 4 feet	Drills 15 to 18 inches; Hills 4 feet	1 to 2	¼ ounce		60 to 80
Vine	7 to 10 feet	Drills 2 to 3 feet; Hills 8 feet	1 to 2	do		120 to 160
Tomato	2 to 3 feet	2 to 3 feet	½ to 1	1/16 ounce	15 to 25	80 to 125
Turnip	15 to 18 inches	2 to 3 inches	¼ to ½	¼ ounce		60 to 80

[1] 50 slips.

TIME OF PLANTING.

Garden crops may be divided into four groups, as follows:

Group 1.—Those vegetables that may be planted some two weeks before the last killing frost. These include cabbage plants, radish, collards, onions (sets), early smooth peas, kale, lettuce (seed in boxes), early potatoes, turnips, and mustard.

Group 2.—Those that may be planted about the date of the last killing frost. These include beets, parsnips, carrots, lettuce, salsify, spinach, wrinkled peas, cauliflower, celery, onions (seed), parsley, lettuce (in open ground), chard, and Chinese cabbage.

Group 3.—Those plants that can not be planted until all danger of frost is past. These include snap beans, sweet corn, okra, and tomatoes (plants).

Group 4.—Heat-loving plants that can not be safely planted until the ground is warm, such as Lima beans, peppers (plants), eggplant, cucumbers, melons, squash, and sweet potatoes. The table gives the dates in the different zones for all garden crops.

Most gardeners are interested in knowing the earliest dates for planting the various crops, as earliness is much desired. It has been found that the earliest safe dates for planting garden crops can be determined from the average dates of the last killing frost in spring.

FIG. 24.—Cowpeas planted as a rotation crop, to be turned under in order to improve the soil.

The map (fig. 31) divides the continental portion of the United States into zones, with a difference between them of about two weeks in the average date of the last killing frost. The average dates of the last killing frost, while a guide in planting, can not be depended upon every year, but are reasonably safe. There is a difference of several days within the zones themselves, owing to difference in elevation, in latitude, and in proximity to bodies of water. The following table gives the earliest safe dates for planting the various vegetables in the open in the different zones illustrated in figure 31.

EARLIEST PLANTING DATES.

Earliest safe dates for planting vegetables in the open in the zones shown in figure 31.

Crop.	Zone A.	Zone B.	Zone C.	Zone D.	Zone E.	Zone F.	Zone G.
Asparagus	(Not grown)	Feb. 15 to Mar. 1	Mar. 1 to 15	Mar. 15 to Apr. 15	Apr. 15 to May 1	May 1 to 15	May 1 to June 1.
Artichoke (Globe)	Mar. 1 to 15	Mar. 15 to Apr. 1	Apr. 1 to 15	Apr. 15 to May 15	May 15 to May 1	(Not grown)	(Not grown).
Artichoke (Jerusalem)	Feb. 1 to 15	Feb. 15 to Mar. 1	Mar. 1 to 15	Mar. 15 to Apr. 1	Apr. 1 to 15	May 1 to 30	Do.
Bean (Lima)	Mar. 1 to 15	Mar. 1 to 15	Apr. 1 to 15	May 1 to 15	May 15 to June 1	May 15 to June 1	May 15 to June 15.
Bean (Snap)	Feb. 15 to Mar. 1	Mar. 1 to 15	Mar. 15 to 30	Apr. 1 to May 1	May 1 to 15	May 15 to June 1	May 15 to June 1.
Beet	Feb. 1 to 15	Feb. 15 to Mar. 1	Mar. 1 to 15	Mar. 15 to Apr. 15	Apr. 15 to May 1	May 1 to 15	
Brussels sprouts	do	do	do	do	do	do	
Cabbage	Jan. 1 to Feb. 1	Jan. 15 to Feb. 15	Feb. 15 to Mar. 1	Mar. 1 to 15	Mar. 15 to Apr. 15	Apr. 15 to May 1	May 1 to May 15.
Carrot	Feb. 1 to 15	Feb. 15 to Mar. 1	Mar. 1 to 15	Mar. 15 to Apr. 15	Apr. 15 to May 1	May 1 to 15	May 1 to June 1.
Cauliflower	do	do	do	do	do	do	Do.
Celery	do	do	do	do	do	do	Do.
Chard	do	do	do	do	do	do	Do.
Collard	Jan. 1 to Feb. 1	Feb. 1 to 15	Feb. 15 to Mar. 1	Mar. 1 to 15	Mar. 15 to Apr. 15	May 1 to June 1	May 15 to June 1.
Corn, sweet	Feb. 15 to Mar. 1	Mar. 1 to 15	Mar. 15 to Apr. 1	Apr. 1 to May 1	Apr. 15 to May 15	May 15 to June 15	June 1 to 15.
Cucumber	Mar. 1 to 15	Mar. 15 to Apr. 1	Apr. 1 to 15	Apr. 15 to May 1	May 1 to June 1	do	
Eggplant	do	do	do	do	do	do	
Garlic	Jan. 1 to Feb. 1	Feb. 1 to 15	Feb. 15 to Mar. 1	Mar. 1 to 15	Mar. 15 to Apr. 15	Apr. 15 to May 1	May 1 to 15.
Kale	do	do	do	do	do	do	Do.
Kohl-rabi	Feb. 1 to 15	Feb. 15 to Mar. 1	Mar. 1 to 15	Mar. 15 to Apr. 15	Apr. 1 to May 1	May 1 to 15	May 15 to June 1.
Lettuce (Head)	do	do	do	do	do	do	Do.
Lettuce (Leaf)	Jan. 1 to Feb. 1	Feb. 1 to 15	Feb. 15 to Mar. 1	Mar. 1 to 15	Mar. 15 to Apr. 15	Apr. 15 to May 15	May 1 to May 15.
Melons	Mar. 1 to 15	Mar. 15 to Apr. 1	Apr. 1 to 15	Apr. 15 to May 1	May 1 to June 1	May 15 to 15	May 15 to June 1.
Mustard	Feb. 1 to 15	Feb. 1 to 15	Mar. 1 to 15	Mar. 15 to Apr. 1	May 1 to May 1	June 1 to 15	June 1 to 15.
Okra, or gumbo	Feb. 15 to Mar. 1	Mar. 1 to Mar. 15	Mar. 15 to 30	Apr. 15 to Apr. 1	May 1 to May 1	May 15 to 15	May 15 to June 1.
Onion, Seed	Feb. 1 to 15	Feb. 15 to Mar. 1	Mar. 1 to 15	Mar. 15 to Apr. 1	Apr. 1 to May 1	May 1 to 15	May 15 to June 1.
Onion, Sets	Jan. 1 to Feb. 1	Feb. 1 to 15	Feb. 15 to Mar. 1	Mar. 1 to 15	Apr. 15 to May 1	Apr. 15 to May 1	May 1 to 15.
Parsley	Feb. 1 to 15	Feb. 15 to Mar. 1	Mar. 1 to 15	Mar. 15 to Apr. 1	Apr. 1 to May 1	May 1 to 15	May 15 to June 1.
Parsnip	do	do	do	do	do	do	Do.
Peas (Smooth)	Jan. 1 to Feb. 1	Feb. 1 to 15	Feb. 15 to Mar. 1	Mar. 1 to 15	Mar. 15 to Apr. 15	Apr. 15 to May 1	May 1 to June 1.
Peas (Wrinkled)	Feb. 1 to 15	Feb. 15 to Mar. 1	Mar. 1 to 15	Mar. 15 to Apr. 1	Apr. 1 to May 1	May 1 to 15	May 15 to June 1.
Peppers	Mar. 1 to 15	Mar. 15 to Apr. 1	Apr. 1 to 15	Apr. 15 to May 1	May 1 to June 1	June 1 to 15	
Potatoes (Irish)	Jan. 1 to Feb. 1	Feb. 1 to 15	Feb. 15 to Mar. 1	Mar. 1 to 15	Mar. 15 to Apr. 15	Apr. 15 to May 1	May 1 to June 1.
Potatoes (Sweet)	Mar. 1 to 15	Mar. 15 to Apr. 1	Apr. 1 to 15	Apr. 15 to May 1	May 1 to June 1	June 1 to 15	
Pumpkin	do	do	do	do	do	do	
Radish	Jan. 1 to Feb. 1	Feb. 1 to 15	Feb. 15 to Mar. 1	Mar. 1 to 15	Mar. 15 to Apr. 15	Apr. 15 to May 1	May 1 to 15.
Rhubarb	(Not grown)	(Not grown)	do	Mar. 15 to Apr. 15	Apr. 15 to May 15	May 15 to June 1	May 15 to June 1.
Salsify	Feb. 1 to 15	Feb. 15 to Mar. 1	Mar. 1 to 15	Mar. 15 to Apr. 15	Apr. 15 to May 1	May 1 to 15	Do.
Spinach	do	do	do	do	do	do	Do.
Squash	Mar. 1 to 15	Mar. 15 to Apr. 1	Apr. 1 to 15	Apr. 15 to May 1	May 1 to June 1	June 1 to June 15	June 1 to 15.
Tomato	do	do	do	do	May 1 to June 1	May 15 to June 15	
Turnip	Jan. 1 to Feb. 1	Feb. 1 to 15	Feb. 15 to Mar. 1	Mar. 1 to 15	Mar. 15 to Apr. 15	Apr. 15 to May 1	May 1 to 15.

THE CITY AND SUBURBAN VEGETABLE GARDEN.

LATEST PLANTING DATES.

Latest safe dates for planting vegetables for the fall garden in the zones[1] shown in figure 32.

Crop.	Zone C.	Zone D.	Zone E.	Zone F.	Zone G.
Bean:					
Bush	Sept. 15	Sept. 1	Aug. 15	Aug. 1	July 15
Pole Lima	...do....	Aug. 1	July 15	July 1	....
Beet	...do....	Sept. 1	Aug. 15	Aug. 1	July 15
Cabbage	Sept. 1	Aug. 15	July 15	July 1	June 15
Carrot	...do....	...do.....	...do.....	...do.....	Do.
Cauliflower	...do....	...do.....	...do.....	...do.....	Do.
Celery	Oct. 1	Sept. 1	Aug. 1	...do.....	May 15
Chard, Swiss	Sept. 15	...do.....	Aug. 15	Aug. 1	July 15
Corn, sweet	Aug. 15	Aug. 1	July 15	July 1	June 15
Cucumber	...do....	...do.....	...do.....	...do.....	....
Eggplant	July 15	July 1	June 15	June 1	....
Kale	Nov. 1	Oct. 1	Sept. 15	Sept. 1	Aug. 15
Lettuce	...do....	Oct. 15	Oct. 1	Sept. 15	Sept. 1
Melons:					
Muskmelon	June 15	June 1	May 15	May 1	....
Watermelon	July 1	July 1	June 15	....	....
Okra	July 15	...do.....	...do.....	June 1	....
Onion:					
Seed	June 15	June 1	May 15	May 1	Apr. 15
Sets	July 15	July 1	June 15	June 1	May 15
Parsley	Nov. 1	Oct. 1	Sept. 1	Aug. 1	July 1
Parsnip	....	....	May 15	May 1	Apr. 15
Pea	Nov. 1	Oct. 1	Sept. 1	Aug. 1	July 15
Peppers	July 15	July 1	June 15	June 1	....
Potatoes:					
Irish	Aug. 15	Aug. 1	July 15	July 1	June 15
Sweet	...do.....	July 15	June 15	May 1	....
Radish	Oct. 15	Oct. 1	Sept. 15	Sept. 1	Aug. 15
Salsify	June 15	June 1	May 15	May 1	Apr. 15
Spinach	Oct. 15	Oct. 1	Sept. 1	Aug. 15	Aug. 1
Squash:					
Bush	Aug. 15	Aug. 1	July 15	July 1	June 15
Vine	July 15	July 1	June 15	June 1	....
Tomato	Aug. 15	July 15	July 1	June 15	....
Turnip	Oct. 15	Oct. 1	Sept. 1	Aug. 1	July 15

[1] Zones A and B are sections in which many vegetables are planted late in the fall to form the winter garden or early spring garden.

Many crops may be used to make a fall garden, and the latest safe dates for planting in the various zones are shown in the above table, which is to be used in connection with the zones shown in figure 32.

SETTING PLANTS.

The soil where plants are to be set should be worked up fine to a depth of several inches, in order to facilitate planting. The plants should be thoroughly watered an hour or so before removing them from the flats or frames, to insure the adherence of the earth to the roots. If the plants have not been transplanted into pots or dirt

FIG. 25.—A flat, or seed box, useful for starting plants to be planted very early in the season.

bands, they should be removed with a ball of earth attached to the roots.

A cloudy day or just before nightfall is the best time to set out plants, though potted plants and plants in dirt bands may be set at any time with good results. The plants should be set a trifle deeper than they were in the seed bed and the soil firmed around each plant from the bottom of the hole to the surface. A trowel or a dibble can be used for making the holes to receive the plants. If water is to be used in setting the plants, it should be poured about the plant when the hole is partially filled with soil. The moist earth is then covered with dry soil, which prevents the rapid evaporation of the moisture.

Cabbage and lettuce plants may be set in the open as soon as the ground can be worked in the spring, but many plants, such as the tomato, pepper, and eggplant, should not be set out until the weather has become warm, as indicated in the table and the zone maps. Some time may be gained by setting the tender plants before danger of frost is over and then protecting them by covering with newspapers, tin cans, berry boxes, or plant covers. These covers may be put over the plants at night when frosts are likely to occur, and if partially removed in the morning they will shade the newly set plants.

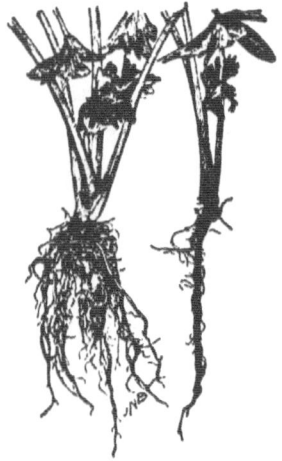

FIG. 23.—Celery plants, showing the effect of transplanting on the root system.

CULTIVATION.

Thorough preparation of the seed bed and good seed properly planted are very essential for successful gardens, but unless the plants are properly cultivated during the season the garden will prove a failure. Cultivation is not entirely for the purpose of killing the weeds, but has as its main object the conserving of soil moisture. Frequent shallow cultivation forms a soil mulch which prevents the loss of moisture, and frequent stirring prevents the growth of weeds. The soil close to the plants should be kept fine and free from weeds, the same as the spaces between the rows. If the cultivation is begun as soon as the plants show and is kept up at regular intervals throughout the season, the work does not become burdensome. If cultivation is given only occasionally, the plants may suffer (fig. 33), and the work is arduous and unsatisfactory. Cultivate the land after every rain, so as to break up the crust that has formed, and give other cultivation as needed to form a soil mulch and keep down weeds.

If the garden has been laid out with long rows and a medium-wide space between the rows, most of the cultivation may be done with a hand cultivator. With such a cultivator the work may be very quickly and efficiently done. In many instances very efficient work can be done with a hoe, but the larger share of the work of cultivating can be performed much more quickly with a hand cultivator.

IRRIGATION.

A good supply of water in the soil is necessary throughout the growing season, to enable the plants to grow vigorously. Many times during long periods of hot, dry weather the supply of moisture in the soil becomes very low, and the plants are so checked in growth that they fail to produce any crop, or at best produce a very poor one. Where a supply of water is available it is often possible to establish

FIG. 27.—A suitable frame for carrying sash for a coldframe or hotbed for a city garden.

an irrigation system which will insure an abundance of water for the plants at a relatively small expense.

Several systems of irrigation are adapted to the garden. An overhead system is probably best. By one such system the water is applied by means of elevated pipes placed at regular intervals over the garden. Nozzles are set in these pipes every 2 feet, and the pressure on the water forces out a fine stream or mist. Water may also be applied to the garden crops by means of a hose by running the water in furrows between the rows or by running the water in tile placed under the soil. The chief factor that must be considered in any system of irrigation is a sufficient supply of water.

CONTROL OF INSECTS AND DISEASES.

Preventive measures are best in the control of insects and diseases. (Fig. 34.) All old vines, cabbage stalks, and the remains of the various crops should be gathered and burned in the autumn. This destroys many insects and to a large measure will prevent the spread of diseases. Following each crop with something not related to it will aid in keeping down insects and diseases. The hand picking of such insects as the Colorado potato beetle is to be recommended. The use of air-slaked lime or dust as a deterrent for insects is effective and inexpensive. The control of garden insects and diseases is fully covered in Farmers' Bulletin 856, "Control of Diseases and Insect Enemies of the Home Vegetable Garden," to which the reader is referred for further information.

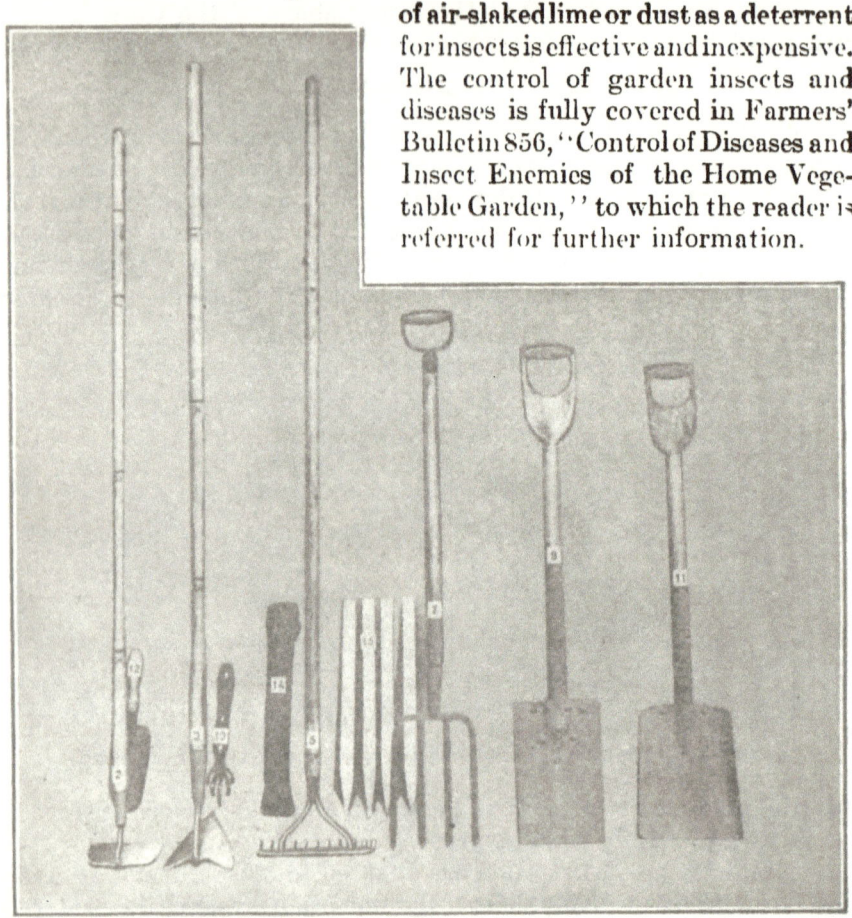

FIG. 28.—A set of garden tools, including the essential implements and a few others. (2) Hoe, (3) heart-shaped furrow hoe, (5) steel-tooth rake, (7) fork, (9) spade, (11) shovel, (12) trowel, (13) scratch weeder, (14) line, (15) stakes. Note that the handles of some of the longer implements are marked off in feet and half feet for convenience in measuring.

SAVING SURPLUS VEGETABLES.

It is just as important to utilize all surplus vegetables as it is to raise them. Those vegetables that are not needed when freshly harvested may be stored, canned, or dried for use during the months when few vegetables are available in the garden. Vegetables may be easily stored with the facilities in or near the ordinary home. Small pits (fig. 35) may be made in the ground, or a portion of the house cellar (fig. 36) may be partitioned off to serve as a storage cellar.

For details of the storage of vegetables, read Farmers' Bulletin 879, entitled "Home Storage of Vegetables."

Fig. 29.—Some small tools useful in the home garden. From left to right they are: Hand weeder, dibble, onion hoe, trowel, and scratch or claw weeder.

Detailed directions for canning vegetables are to be found in Farmers' Bulletins 839 [1] and 853 [2] and for drying in Farmers' Bulletin 841.[3]

DIRECTIONS FOR GROWING VEGETABLE CROPS.

ASPARAGUS.

Asparagus should be grown in every home garden where it will thrive, because it is one of the earliest vegetables and is a valuable addition to the spring diet. The soil for asparagus should be made quite rich by the application of partly rotted manure before the plants are set. As soon as danger from hard frosts is over, the seeds of asparagus may be sown in the rows where the plants are to remain. Soaking the seed in hot water for an hour or two before planting will hasten germination.

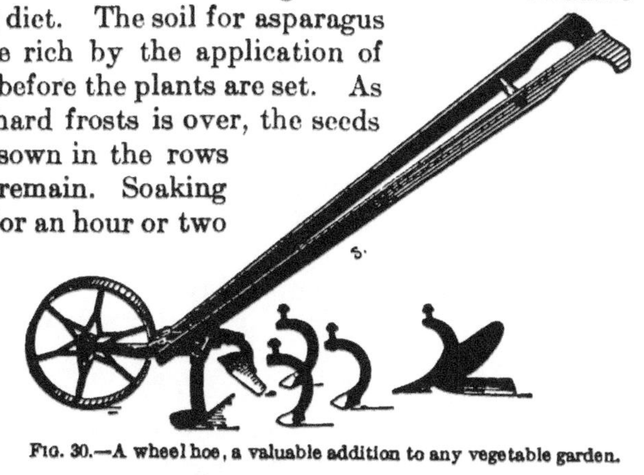

The seedlings should be thinned to stand 15 inches apart in the row. Quicker results can be secured,

Fig. 30.—A wheel hoe, a valuable addition to any vegetable garden.

---

[1] Entitled "Home Canning by the One-Period Cold-Pack Method Taught to Canning Club Members in the Northern and Western States."

[2] Entitled "Home Canning of Fruits and Vegetables as Taught to Canning Club Members in the Southern States."

[3] Entitled "Drying Fruits and Vegetables in the Home, with Recipes for Cooking."

however, by buying roots from some seedsman or dealer. The roots may be planted in the autumn or early spring. Before setting the plants, the soil should be loosened deeply by spading or by the use of a subsoil plow. The roots may be set in a solid bed 1 foot apart each way. Cover the roots to the depth of 4 or 5 inches. The bed should receive a dressing of manure or fertilizer each year, preferably in the autumn.

No shoots should be removed the first year the plants are set in the permanent bed, and the cutting season should be short the second year. After the bed is well established, with proper care and fertilizing it should last indefinitely. During the cutting season, all of the shoots, even those too small for use, should be removed.

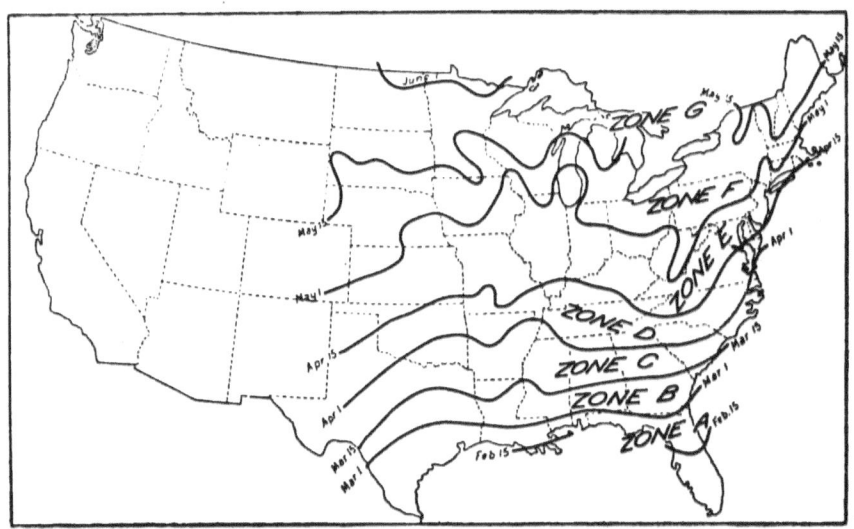

FIG. 31.—Outline map of the United States, showing zones based on the average date of the last killing frost in spring. The time of planting for the various vegetables is determined for every section by the dates given on this map.

After this, the tops should be allowed to grow until late in the season, when they should be removed and burned and the soil between the rows cultivated. Apply a dressing of manure after cultivation and allow it to remain on the bed.

Varieties recommended: Palmetto, Reading Giant, and Giant Argenteuil.

BEANS.

Beans will not withstand much cold, so they should not be planted until danger of frost is past and the ground begins to warm up. The first planting should be made as soon as the ground is reasonably warm, and other plantings may be made at intervals of ten days or two weeks until hot weather sets in. Beans for the fall garden should be planted in late summer, and successive plantings may be made at the intervals suggested until about eight weeks before time for the first frost in the autumn.

Bush beans should be planted to stand 2 to 3 inches apart in rows 20 to 24 inches apart. Among the best varieties of bush beans are the Stringless Green Pod, Refugee, Hodson's Kidney Wax, Currie's Rustproof Wax, and Wardwell's Kidney Wax.

Lima beans, both pole and bush, should be grown in the garden (fig. 37). These should be planted after all danger of frost is over and the soil is warm. Plant the pole beans 8 to 10 seeds in a hill and thin to 3 or 4 after the plants become established. The hills should be 4 or 5 feet apart. For bush Lima beans, plant 5 or 6 inches apart in rows 30 to 36 inches apart.

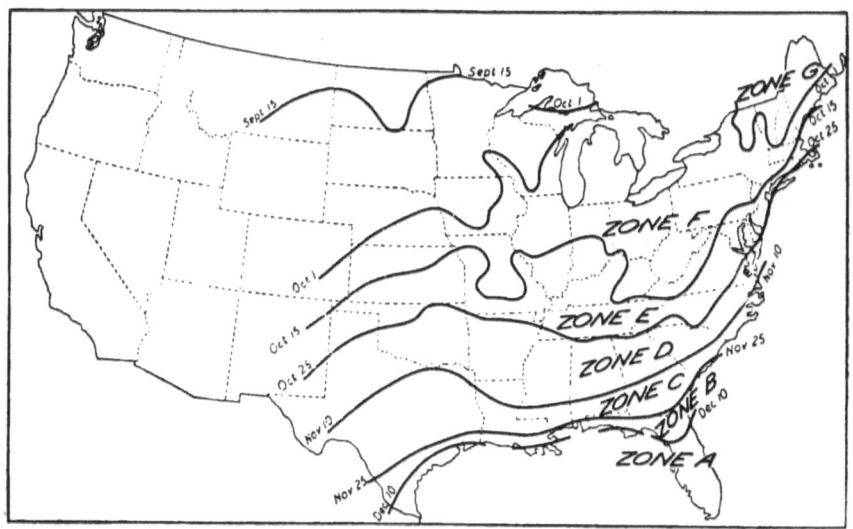

Fig. 32.—Outline map of the United States, showing zones based on the average date of the first killing frost in the autumn. The latest safe dates for planting vegetables in the autumn are determined by the dates given on this map.

When planting beans of any kind the seed should not be covered over 2 inches, and on heavy soils they should not be covered more than 1¼ to 1½ inches.

Varieties recommended: Seibert's Pole Lima, Carpinteria Lima, and King of the Limas are good varieties of pole Lima beans, and Fordhook Bush Lima, Dreer's Bush Lima, and Henderson's Bush Lima are good varieties of the bush type.

BEETS.

Beets (fig. 38) can be planted as soon as the ground can be worked up mellow in the spring, even before the ground has become warm. Sow the seeds in drills 14 to 18 inches apart, covering to the depth of about 1 inch. As soon as the plants are well up, thin them to stand 4 to 5 inches apart. Make two or three plantings, so as to have a continuous supply of young, tender beets throughout the season. In many sections of the South beets may be left in the ground through the winter, to be pulled when wanted.

Varieties recommended: Crosby's Egyptian, Bassano, Early Eclipse, and Early Blood Turnip.

CABBAGE.

In Florida and the Gulf coast region of the other Southern States cabbage seed may be sown in the open any time from September to January. Along the Atlantic coast, from Charleston, S. C., to Florida, seed may be sown in the open in October. In all other sections of the South hotbeds or coldframes should be used for starting the plants.

For spring and early-summer cabbage the following varieties are recommended: Jersey Wakefield, Charleston Wakefield, Allhead Early, and Succession. The Copenhagen Market, a new variety, has given excellent results in many localities and is well worthy of a trial. The Flat Dutch and Danish Ball Head are desirable late varieties for the Northern States.

In most sections of the South it is not advisable to grow cabbage during midsummer, but a fall crop should be grown. The same varieties may be grown in the autumn as in the spring, but it is usually desirable to plant larger varieties, such as Flat Dutch or Danish Ball Head. Seed for the fall crop should be planted in a cool loca-

FIG. 33.—A poorly kept garden, involving a waste of time, energy, and seed.

tion in late summer and the plants set out as soon as they reach the proper size and the soil contains sufficient moisture to start growth. Cabbage plants should be set 14 to 18 inches apart in rows 30 to 36 inches apart. The earlier varieties, which grow small heads, are usually set closer than the later ones.

CARROT.

The soil and cultural requirements of carrots are practically the same as for beets. Carrot seed, however, should not be planted so deep as beet seed, and the plants can be allowed to grow closer together in the row (fig. 39). Carrots may be dug in the autumn and stored in banks or cellars, or they may be left in the ground to be harvested as needed.

Varieties recommended: Half-Long Danvers, Early Scarlet Horn, and Chantenay.

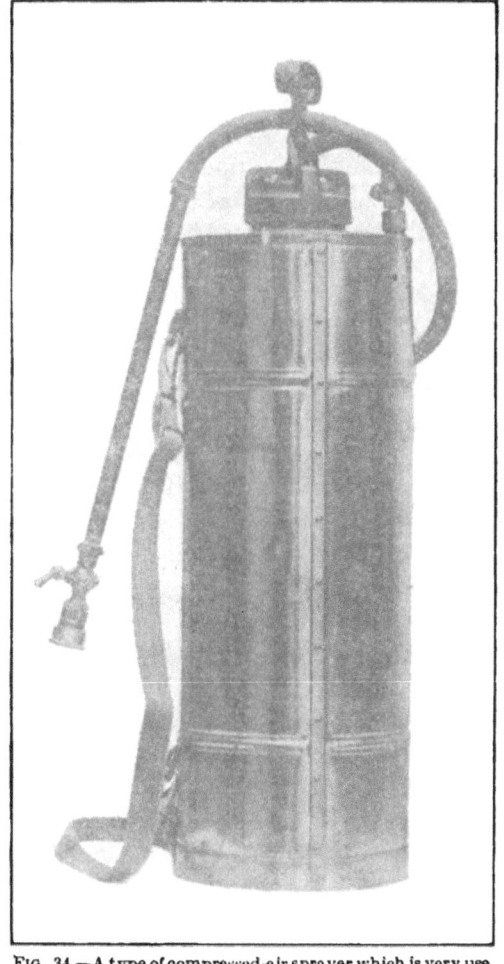

FIG. 34.—A type of compressed-air sprayer which is very useful in a home garden.

CAULIFLOWER.

Cauliflower thrives best on a rich, moist soil. The culture of this crop is about the same as for cabbage, but it will not withstand as much frost. In order to secure bleached heads it is necessary to protect them from the sun (fig. 40). The usual practice is to tie the leaves together over the heads.

Varieties recommended: Early Snowball and Dwarf Erfurt are the varieties of cauliflower most commonly grown.

CELERY.

In the lower South celery is grown as a fall crop, as it will not mature during hot weather. The seed is sown in a cool, shady place in late summer and the plants set out in the autumn as soon as the soil becomes moist. The seed should be sown in rows and covered lightly (not more than one-eighth of an inch) or sown broadcast and covered with burlap, straw, or some other material, to prevent the loss of moisture while the seed is germinating. It will be necessary to water the seed bed often during dry weather.

In the North or upper South celery may be grown in the spring or in the autumn. As a spring crop, the seed should be started in a hotbed during the winter so that the plants may mature before midsummer. Celery does not bleach well in hot weather, but rots when banked or boarded for bleaching.

Set the celery plants 6 inches apart in rows 3 feet apart for horse cultivation, or 18 to 24 inches apart when hand cultivation is to be employed.

Celery requires a deep, rich, moist soil and frequent shallow cultivation. When grown as a fall crop celery may be planted after some other crop, such as peas, beans, cabbage, lettuce, or radishes. When

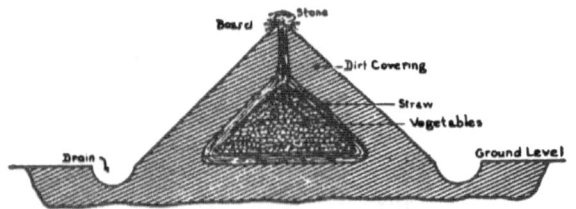

Fig. 35.—A method for the storage of root crops. Cross section of a storage pit containing Irish potatoes. During severely cold weather the dirt covering may be supplemented by manure, straw, etc.

the celery plants are nearly grown a little soil should be drawn around the base to hold the plants in place. About two weeks before they are wanted for the table the bleaching should begin. Soil, boards, or paper may be used for bleaching, but soil should be employed only when the weather is cool. When soil is to be used for bleaching, the rows should be 4 feet apart. Some quick-maturing crop could be grown between the rows of celery to make use of the space up to the time for bleaching.

Varieties recommended: Golden Self-Blanching, Columbia, and White Plume.

COLLARD.

A group of nonheading cabbages differing slightly from kale, but withstanding summer heat better than either kale or cabbage, is extensively grown throughout the South under the name of Georgia collards. Collards do not make a true head, but form a rosette of leaves, which are very tender. The culture and uses of this plant are the same as those of cabbage and kale.

CHARD, SWISS.

Swiss chard is a beet plant that has been developed for the foliage instead of for the root (see fig. 38). The leaves continue to develop throughout the season and are picked off when small. Two or three of the central shoots are always left to carry on the growth. Chard is planted like beets in rows 12 to 14 inches apart and gradually thinned out so the plants stand 12 inches apart in the row. The seed is sown at the same time as beets and the leaves are ready for use in about five weeks. The fleshy leafstalk is very often used the same as asparagus.

Swiss chard is especially useful in the small garden because the leaves can be used for greens in place of spinach and a sufficient number of plants occupy only a small fraction of the space needed to raise the required supply of spinach.

Giant Lucullus is the variety commonly grown.

CORN, SWEET.

Sweet corn should be planted on rich land and cultivated the same as field corn (fig. 41). Plant the seed as soon as the soil is warm in the spring, and make successive plantings every two or three weeks until late summer.

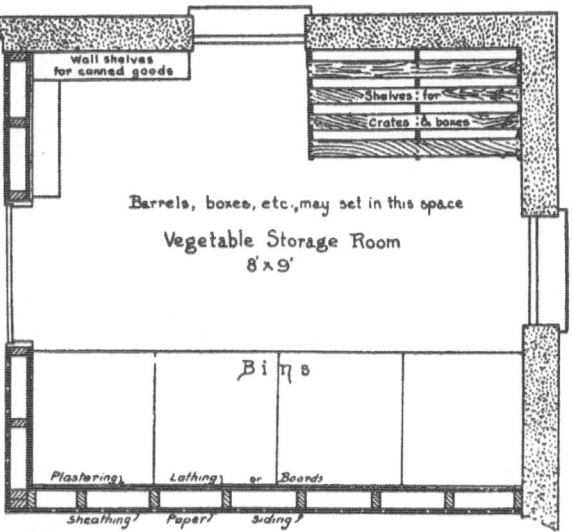

FIG. 36.—A plan showing how a storage room may be made in the cellar of a dwelling. The arrangement of the shelving and bins may be changed to suit conditions. While the construction of the wall may be varied, it must be tight.

The same results can be obtained to some extent by planting early, medium, and late varieties. Plant the seeds about 2 inches deep in drills 3 feet apart, and thin to a single stalk every 10 to 14 inches.

The flavor of sweet corn depends upon the stage of maturity and the method of handling the product from the plant to the table. Sweet corn loses its flavor very rapidly after being removed from the stalk. It should, therefore, be picked only a few hours, and preferably a few minutes, in advance of the time when it is to be placed in the pot.

Varieties recommended: For early corn Golden Bantam and Adams Early are suggested, and for medium and late varieties Black Mexican, Country Gentleman, and Stowell's Evergreen. The last-named variety has the largest ears and is the most productive.

Fig. 37.—A tennis backstop forming a good support for Lima beans. The yield from these vines was 25 quarts of shelled beans.

CUCUMBERS.

The soil for cucumbers should be rich, and it is a good plan to apply well-rotted manure under the rows or hills. If planted in rows, open the furrow and scatter the manure along the furrow, turning fresh soil over the manure before planting the seeds. If the seeds are planted in hills, confine the application of manure to the area occupied by the hills.

As cucumbers are easily injured by cold, it is not advisable to plant until all danger of frost is over and the ground has begun to warm up. For very early cucumbers the seeds should be planted in a hotbed in old strawberry boxes or plant bands or directly in the soil of the bed. By starting the plants in hotbeds the cucumbers will be ready for the table two or three weeks earlier than if started in the open. For the main crop, drill the seed in rows 5 feet apart, and after the plants reach a height of 3 or 4 inches thin them to stand 12 to 18 inches apart in the row, or plant the seeds in hills 4 feet apart each way and thin to two or three plants to the hill.

Cucumbers should be given frequent shallow cultivation until the vines fill most of the space between the rows; after this very little attention will be needed, except to pull out any weeds by hand. Do not allow any fruit to ripen on the vines until the end of the picking season, as new fruits will not form while older ones are ripening.

Young cucumber plants are often destroyed by the cucumber beetle. It is possible to protect the plants by covering them with small wooden frames over which mosquito netting has been stretched.

THE CITY AND SUBURBAN VEGETABLE GARDEN. 43

Air-slaked lime sprinkled over the small plants is an added protection against the cucumber beetle.

Varieties recommended: White Spine, Davis Perfect, and Emerald.

EGGPLANT.

The plants for this crop should be started in a hotbed or in a box in the house about two months before time for planting in the garden. The plants should not be set in the field until after all danger of frost has passed and the ground has become quite warm. Set the plants 18 to 24 inches apart in rows 3 feet apart, and give clean, shallow cultivation to keep the plants growing rapidly. A dozen good,

FIG. 38.—Beets and Swiss chard, excellent crops in any home garden.

healthy plants will supply enough fruit for the average-sized family throughout the season.

Varieties recommended: New York Improved Purple and Black Beauty.

GARLIC.

Garlic is propagated by separating the bulbs into the small bulblets, or cloves, and planting these separately in rows 12 to 14 inches apart and from 3 to 4 inches apart in the row, either in the autumn or spring. In other respects the cultivation is the same as for onions. The mature bulbs are pulled and left on the ground until the tops are dry, when they are gathered, braided together, and hung in a shed to cure. Garlic is used for flavoring purposes.

KALE.

Kale is a very hardy crop and can be grown in the open during the winter in practically all sections of the South. In the more northern sections it is grown either as a spring or fall crop. Sow the seed in

FIG. 39.—A patch of excellent carrots in a city garden.

drills 18 inches apart, and thin the plants to stand 4 or 6 inches apart in the row. Seed for the spring crop may be sown as soon as the soil can be conveniently worked. Seed for the fall or winter crop may be sown in early autumn.

Varieties recommended: Dwarf Curled, Tall Scotch, and Siberian.

KOHL-RABI.

Kohl-rabi belongs to the same class as cabbage and cauliflower, but does not resemble either. The edible portion is the swollen stem, which resembles a turnip, but which is formed above ground. Kohl-rabi should be grown both in the spring and in the autumn. Sow

FIG. 40.—A row of cauliflower in a vacant lot garden. The leaves are tied at the top to keep the heads white.

the seed in drills and thin the plants to 6 inches apart in the row. The rows should be 18 inches apart. The fleshy stems should be used while fresh and tender, as they become tough and stringy within a short time.

Variety recommended: White Vienna.

LETTUCE.

Lettuce thrives best during cool weather, so it should be planted in the spring and autumn. In order that the leaves or head may be crisp, the crop should be forced and successive plantings made ten days or two weeks apart. In the lower South lettuce can be grown in the open during the winter, but in the North hotbeds or coldframes must be used.

When grown in the garden, the seeds should be sown in rows 14 to 16 inches apart and the plants thinned to the desired distance. The heading type should be thinned to stand 8 inches apart in the row, but with the loose-leaf type the plants may be grown close together and thinned as needed for the table. For a very early crop, start the plants in the hotbed or coldframe and transplant the young plants to the garden as soon as hard freezes are over. Give the plants frequent shallow cultivations.

Varieties recommended: Grand Rapids and Black-Seeded Simpson for loose-leaf lettuce, and Big Boston, Hanson, and California Cream Butter for head lettuce.

MELONS.

Muskmelon.—The culture of the muskmelon is the same as for the cucumber, except that the plants are usually given more space. Plant 8 to 10 seeds in a hill, spacing the hills 6 feet apart each way After the plants become established, thin out all but four of the best ones. Another method is to sow in drills 6 feet apart and thin to single plants 18 to 24 inches apart.

FIG. 41.—Corn grown in a lot utilized as a home garden.

Varieties recommended: Rocky Ford, Netted Gem, Emerald Gem, Paul Rose, and Osage.

Watermelon.—The cultivation of the watermelon is the same as for the cucumber and muskmelon, except that the plants require more space. Plant watermelon seeds in rows 8 to 10 feet apart and thin to single plants 3 feet apart, or plant in hills 8 to 10 feet apart each way.

Varieties recommended: Kleckley Sweets, Florida Favorite, Georgia Rattlesnake, and Tom Watson.

MUSTARD.

Mustard is used largely for greens and can be grown in early spring and late autumn. The seeds for the spring crop should be sown as soon as the soil can be put into condition. For the fall crop, sow the seeds in the late summer or early autumn in drills about 1 foot apart. As the plants require but a short time in which to reach edible maturity, frequent sowings should be made.

Varieties recommended: Giant Ostrich Plume and Large-Leaved Curled.

OKRA, OR GUMBO.

Okra is a plant that is especially desirable in southern gardens. Sow seeds in the open after danger of frost is over and the soil becomes quite warm. The rows should be 3 to 4 feet apart for dwarf varieties and 4 to 5 feet for the tall kinds. Sow the seed a few inches apart in the row and thin the plants to 18 inches to 2 feet apart. Give frequent shallow cultivations until the plants are nearly grown.

The pods are the part of the plant used for food and should be gathered while still crisp and tender. If the pods are removed so as to allow none to ripen, the plants will continue to bear until killed by frost.

Varieties recommended: White Velvet, Dwarf Green Prolific, Perkins Mammoth, Long Podded, and Lady Finger.

ONIONS.

For very early bunch onions it is the common practice to plant sets in drills 12 to 14 inches apart and 2 to 3 inches apart in the row. In the South the sets may be put out in the autumn or as early in the spring as the land can be prepared. In the North the sets are put out as soon as the ground can be worked in the spring.

For dry onions, sow the seed thickly in drills about 12 to 14 inches apart in the spring as soon as danger from hard frosts is over. For early bulbs the seed may be planted in a hotbed or coldframe and the young plants transplanted to the open when conditions are favorable. Plants 4 or 5 inches high are of good size for transplanting.

Onions require frequent shallow cultivations and it may be necessary to resort to hand weeding. When the tops begin to die and the bulbs are full grown, the onions should be pulled and left in the field for a few days to dry. Then the tops should be clipped off and the bulbs placed in crates or bags and stored in a well-ventilated place to cure.

Early green onions may also be produced from the Multiplier or Potato varieties planted in the autumn. The large bulbs of these onions contain a number of "hearts", or buds, and if planted will produce a number of small onions. The small onions have but one heart and will produce large bulbs. A few large bulbs should be planted each year to produce sets for fall planting.

The Top, or Tree, onion produces a number of bulblets on top of the stem. These small bulbs can be planted in the autumn and will produce onions the following spring.

Varieties recommended: Southport White Globe, Southport Red Globe, Southport Yellow Globe, Danvers, Red Wethersfield, Australian Brown, and Prize Taker. In some sections of the South the Creole is grown and the Louisiana, or Red Creole, is a popular variety. The Bermuda is a good type of mild-flavored onion and is a desirable type to grow in the South. The important varieties of the Bermuda are Crystal Wax, White Bermuda, and Red Bermuda.

OYSTER PLANT. See SALSIFY.

PARSLEY.

Parsley is used mainly for garnishing meats, but can be used for flavoring soups and other foods. Sow parsley seed thickly in a drill or sow broadcast and cover lightly, either in the autumn or early spring. A space a yard square will be sufficient for parsley.

Varieties recommended: Plain Leaved and Double Curled.

PARSNIP.

Sow parsnip seed in the spring as soon as danger of hard frosts is over, in drills 14 to 16 inches apart. Thin the plants to stand 3 inches apart in the rows. The cultivation of parsnips should be about the same as for beets and carrots. A crop may be planted in midsummer for winter use, and the roots may be left in the ground through the winter or until needed, as freezing is believed to improve the flavor of parsnips. If it is desired to plow the garden before the parsnips are disposed of, they may be dug and stored in a cool place or buried in banks or pits.

Varieties recommended: Hollow Crown and Student.

PEAS.

Garden peas, sometimes called English peas, are not injured by light frosts, so they should be planted as soon as the soil can be put in order in the spring. The first plantings should be of small-growing, quick-maturing varieties, such as Alaska, First and Best, and Gradus, which do not require supports. These varieties should be followed by the large wrinkled type of peas, such as Champion of England, Telephone, and Prize Taker. The large-growing varieties should be supported on brush, on strings attached to stakes driven in the ground, or on wire netting. In order to have a continuous supply of peas, plantings should be made every 10 days or two weeks until warm weather. Peas should be planted in late summer and autumn for the fall garden, for which the early varieties are more desirable than the late ones.

Peas should be planted about 2 to 3 inches deep in rows 3 to 4 feet apart. Some gardeners, however, follow the practice of planting in double rows 6 inches apart, with the ordinary space of 3 to 4 feet between these pairs of rows. This is a good practice with varieties requiring support, as the supports can be placed in the narrow space between the rows.

Varieties recommended: Alaska, First and Best, Gradus, Telephone, Champion of England, and Prize Taker.

PEPPERS.

Seeds of peppers should be sown in a hotbed or in a box in the house about eight weeks before time for setting the plants in the garden. The plants are tender and should not be transplanted until the ground is warm and all danger of frost is past. Set the plants 15 to 18 inches apart in rows $2\frac{1}{2}$ to 3 feet apart. The cultivation and treatment of peppers should be the same as that of tomatoes and eggplants. There is a large number of varieties of peppers, including the sweet kinds and the hot peppers.

Varieties recommended: Ruby King, Chinese Giant, Sweet Spanish, and Bell or Bull Nose, of the sweet peppers; Long Red Cayenne, Tabasco, and Red Cluster, of the hot types.

POTATOES.

Irish or white potatoes.—A small area of early potatoes should be grown in the garden, but the main crop should be grown elsewhere. Early potatoes should be planted as soon as the ground can be prepared to good advantage. In Florida, potatoes are usually planted in December, while in other sections of the lower South they are planted in January. In the upper South early potatoes are usually planted in February, but in the Northern States they are not planted until March or April.

Potatoes are planted 12 to 14 inches apart in rows $2\frac{1}{2}$ to 3 feet apart and covered to the depth of about 4 inches. Potatoes planted during hot weather sohuld be covered 6 inches deep unless they have been sprouted before planting. The furrows are opened and the potatoes dropped, one piece in a place, in the bottom of the furrow. As it requires two or three weeks for potatoes to come up, it is important that'they be cultivated as soon as the row can be followed. If a crust forms before the potatoes come up, a rake should be run over the ground to loosen the surface of the soil. Hand cultivators should be used for the main cultivation, but at the last cultivation the soil may be worked up around the plants to hold them erect and to protect the tubers from the sun.

After digging the early potatoes they should be kept in a cool, dry place during the hot weather of summer. In the South it is better to grow a fall crop rather than to try to keep the spring crop through the summer and winter. Fall-grown potatoes can be kept in a dry cellar, in a pit, or in any building where the temperature can be controlled. Irish potatoes keep best in a cool temperature, but should not be allowed to reach the freezing point. It is best not to allow the temperature to fall below 36° F.

Varieties recommended: Irish Cobbler, Bliss Red Triumph, and Early Rose are good, early potatoes. Where only one variety is to be grown, the Irish Cobbler is recommended. In the South the same varieties may be grown for the fall crop, or the Green Mountain, which is a late variety, may be used. In the North the Green Mountain and Rural New Yorker are commonly used for late varieties.

RADISH.

The radish is quite hardy and may be grown in the open all winter in the South and in coldframes in the North. Sow the seed in the open ground as soon as danger of hard frosts is over, or in coldframes whenever space is available. In the open, sow the seed in drills 12 to 15 inches apart and thin the plants to 1 inch apart. Successive plantings should be made every 10 days or two weeks until hot weather comes and again in the autumn when the weather begins to get cool.

Varieties recommended: There are three types of radishes—turnip shaped, olive shaped, and long. Of the turnip shaped, the best varieties are the Scarlet Globe and Scarlet Turnip. The best of the olive-shaped sorts are the French Breakfast and Early Scarlet. The Long Scarlet Chartier, Long White Spanish, and Icicle are the best varieties of the long type.

RHUBARB.

Rhubarb can be grown in the North and the upper South, but can not be grown satisfactorily in the lower South. For home use it is best to buy roots from a dealer rather than to grow plants from seed. Ten to twelve good hills are sufficient for the average family.

Set the roots 3 to 4 feet apart along the garden fence and manure heavily. The treatment suggested for asparagus is satisfactory for rhubarb. Do not allow the plants to go to seed.

SALSIFY, OR VEGETABLE OYSTER.

Sow seeds of salsify at the same time and in the same manner as those of parsnips and carrots. An ounce of seed will plant a 100-foot row and will be sufficient for an average family. After the plants are up, thin them to about 2 inches apart in the row. Salsify may be dug and stored the same as parsnips and carrots or left in the soil until needed. It is a biennial, and if the roots are not dug they will produce seed the second season. Salsify deserves more general cultivation, as it is one of the most desirable root crops.

The Sandwich Island is the variety commonly grown.

SPINACH.

Spinach is one of the best crops grown for greens and should be found in every large home garden. It can be grown in the open throughout the autumn and winter in all sections along the coast from Norfolk, Va., south and in the lower tier of Southern States. In the lower portions of the northern sections it requires protection during the coldest weather. Two or three inches of hay, straw, or leaves will be a satisfactory protection. The seed planted in the autumn will furnish greens through the winter and early spring in the warmer sections. In the Northern States the crop is usually grown in the spring.

Sow the seeds of spinach in drills 12 to 15 inches apart at the rate of 1 ounce to 100 feet of row. Three or four ounces of seed will produce enough greens for the average family. In gathering, the entire plant is removed. The large plants are selected first and the smaller or later ones are thus given room to develop.

The Savoy is the variety most commonly grown.

SQUASH.

There are two types of squashes, the bush varieties and the running varieties. The bush varieties should be planted in hills 4 feet apart each way and the running varieties 8 to 10 feet apart each way. Squashes are prolific, and the supply for the average family will ordinarily be furnished by five or six hills of each sort. Squash seed should not be planted until after danger of frost is over and the soil is quite warm. The cultivation and care of squashes should be the same as that given cucumbers or muskmelons.

Varieties recommended: The varieties of summer squash commonly grown are Pattypan, Summer Crookneck, and Vegetable Marrow. Of the winter squashes the Hubbard and Golden Hubbard are among the best.

TOMATOES.

To get a crop of early tomatoes the seed should be started about eight weeks before time for setting the plants in the field. In the South the plants can be grown in coldframes covered with canvas or cotton cloth, but in the North a hotbed should be employed. When only a few plants are needed the seed may be sown in a shallow box in the house. For the best results in growing tomatoes the young plants should be transplanted as soon as they reach a height of 1½ to 2 inches. Transplant them to stand 2 inches apart each way in a hotbed, coldframe, or box in the house. When the plants begin to crowd, it is a good plan to transplant them to flower pots, plant bands, old strawberry boxes, or tin cans from which the bottoms and tops have been melted.

Tomato plants should be set in the open as soon as danger of frost has passed. If the plants are to be pruned to one or two stems and tied to stakes, they should be set 18 inches apart in rows 3 feet apart. If the plants are not pruned or staked, they may be planted 3 feet apart in rows 4 feet apart. It is advisable, however, to prune and train to stakes, especially for the early crop, as plants so treated will be healthier and more easily cultivated and will produce fruit which is earlier and more uniform in size and shape than that produced by plants which have not been trained and pruned. Soon after setting the plants in the field a stake should be driven near each plant, to which it may be tied. Care should be exercised to tie the plant so that it will not be injured by the string. A good plan is to loop the string around the stake and tie it under a leaf stem. Go over the patch once every week or ten days and remove all shoots starting in the axils of the leaves.

Varieties recommended: For early tomatoes, Earliana or Chalk's Early Jewel is recommended, preferably the former. For medium and late varieties, the following are suggested: Greater Baltimore, Red Rock, Globe, Beauty, Acme, and Stone. The Stone is usually preferred for canning.

TURNIPS.

The turnip should be grown both as a spring and as a fall crop. For the spring crop, plant as early as the condition of the soil will permit, and for the fall crop sow the seed in late summer or early autumn. Sow the seed thickly in rows 15 to 18 inches apart, and as the plants reach a height of 4 or 5 inches begin thinning, using the young plants for greens. For good roots thin the plants to about 3 inches apart in the row. Cultivate turnips the same as carrots and parsnips. Turnips may be left in the ground until needed for the table, pulled and stored in a cellar, or buried in banks or pits.

Varieties recommended: Purple-Top Globe, White Globe, Seven Top, White Milan, and Yellow Aberdeen.

Rutabaga.—Rutabagas may be grown as a fall and winter crop to very good advantage. They are planted the same as turnips, except that they require more room and a longer period of growth.

The Purple Top is the most common variety of rutabaga.

○

www.ingramcontent.com/pod-product-compliance
Lightning Source LLC
Chambersburg PA
CBHW021133080526
44587CB00012B/1264